I0884606

Look Who's Here

This book belongs to:

....

Text by Louise Shanagher
Design and illustration by Rose Finerty

Look Who's Here

THE LILLIPUT PRESS
62–63 Sitric Road, Arbour Hill
Dublin 7, Ireland
www.lilliputpress.ie

Copyright © 2018 Louise Shanagher and Rose Finerty
ISBN 978 1 84351 735 1

10 9 8 7 6 5 4 3 2 1

All rights reserved. No part of the text is to be construed as medical advice. No part of this publication may be reproduced in any form or by any means without the prior permission of the publisher.
A CIP record for this title is available from The British Library.

This is the third book in the Mindfully Me series.

Printed in Spain by Castuera

the arts council an chomhairle ealaíon funding literature artscouncil.ie

A Note for Parents and Teachers

This book helps children to view their feelings as friendly visitors who stop by for a while but will soon be on their way again. The story and workbook pages guide children in understanding and managing difficult emotions, encouraging them to relate to their feelings with mindfulness, self-compassion and kindness.

How to use this book

When reading this book to children, ask them to imagine that their feelings are visitors, just like the characters in the story. These 'feeling' visitors will stay for a while but will soon move on, making space for a new visitor to come along. Ask the children what feeling is visiting them at the moment and how this feels inside them. You can suggest words like 'heavy', 'fizzing', 'butterflies', 'tingling' and 'tight' to help the children describe the sensations.

Remind the children that all feelings are OK and, although some emotions are uncomfortable, they are all important and will pass in time. You can encourage the children to have a curious, friendly attitude towards their feelings and to use the techniques mentioned in the story, particularly when uncomfortable ones come to visit. Emphasize the importance of talking about and expressing feelings and encourage the children to notice the difference in their bodies when they express their feelings and when they try to contain them.

Mindfulness

This story promotes a mindful attitude in relation to feelings. Mindfulness is the practice of deliberately and non-judgmentally paying attention to the present moment. By taking deep breaths and being aware of themselves, children can support and ground themselves when uncomfortable feelings come to visit.

Self-compassion

Rather than viewing feelings as enemies or something to be avoided, this story encourages children to focus on themselves and their emotions with kindness and acceptance. Children can be encouraged to give themselves a hug and to speak in a kind, gentle way to themselves and their feelings.

Identifying and expressing feelings

This story helps children identify and express their emotions. The workbook pages encourage children to express emotions creatively by talking, writing, drawing and colouring.

How to use the workbook pages

You can use the workbook pages to reinforce the message of the story and help initiate conversations about thoughts, feelings and experiences with children. Try to create an accepting and non-judgmental atmosphere. Reassure the children that there are no right or wrong answers: all our thoughts and feelings are OK. By talking about them, we can get to know ourselves better. Children can write or draw their answers into a 'mindfulness diary' that can be used every day as a way for children to express their feelings.

Younger children may be more comfortable talking through their responses rather than writing or drawing them. The Mindfully Me series is aimed at children aged four and up, and additional ideas for activities for different age groups up to eight years old can be found at **www.loulourose.net**.

Tips for teachers

This book is aligned with the Irish primary schools' SPHE curriculum and the Aistear framework. This book links particularly well with the strand 'Myself' and the strand units 'Self Identity' and 'Growing and Changing'. For tips on how to use this book in the classroom, lesson plans and other resources, please visit **www.loulourose.net**.

When my feelings came to visit,
I used to be a little rude.
I'd tell them to be quiet,
that I wasn't in the mood.

I wouldn't let my feelings in,
I'd tell them, 'Go away!'
Though in the end it didn't work –
my feelings always stayed.

Oh, no, Worried Walter,
will you please just go away?
Can't you see I'm busy
and my friend is here to play?

Not you, Shy Cecil!
It's really not the time.
Everybody's watching
and it's time to say my line.

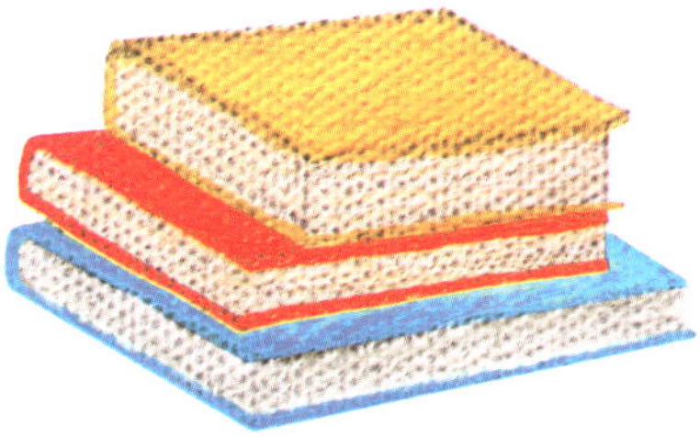

Then one day, I heard a voice,
it came from deep inside.

Yes, my feelings are my friends,
just here to visit for a while.
I say, 'Welcome!' to my feelings now
and greet them with a smile.

Hello there, Nervous Nelly,
how are you today?
I take a big deep breath,
I know that I'm OK.

Welcome, Sad Sandrina,
do you need a little cry?
I give myself a hug,
and know that I am fine.

Oh, Angry Angelina,
is there something wrong?
I talk about my feelings
and know that I am strong.

So, when your feelings come to visit,
remember that you're safe.
Be patient with them all,
give them time and space.

When your feelings come to visit,
remember to be kind.
They'll soon be on their way again,
they're only passing by.

Activity 3A

All About Me

Circle or colour the feeling that is visiting you now or draw a new feeling in the box. Remember, there is no right or wrong way to feel: all our feelings are OK.

Body Feelings

Write, draw or tell someone how you feel in your body when these feelings come to visit.

Worried Walter

Angry Angelina

Sad Sandrina

Activity 3C

When Feelings Visit

Write, draw or tell someone some tricks you can use to help you when your feelings come to visit.